DI010741

# Skin

by Jennifer Boothroyd

first step nonfiction

Lerner Publications Company · Minneapolis

**Skin** is a covering around an animal's body.

Many kinds of animals
have skin.

Frogs have skin.   People
have skin.

Skin can have other
coverings on top of it.

5

Polar bears have skin under their fur.

Birds have skin under their feathers.

Skin can be dry and rough.

Skin can be slimy and smooth.

Human skin has many
shades.

Skin helps animals hide.

This snake is **camouflaged**.
It is hard to see.

Skin **protects** animals.

Some animals have very thick skin.

It stops them from getting
hurt badly.

Old skin can fall off in large
pieces or in small flakes.

Animals need skin to **survive**.

# Our Skin

Our skin is made of three layers.  You can see the top layer.  This layer has holes called pores.  Sweat comes out of these pores. Farther down is the middle layer.  Hair starts in this layer.  It grows through the top layer.  Sweat and oil are made in the middle layer. Nerves send messages of pain or touch to your brain.  Nerves are also in the middle layer. The lowest layer mostly has fat and blood vessels.

# The Layers of Human Skin

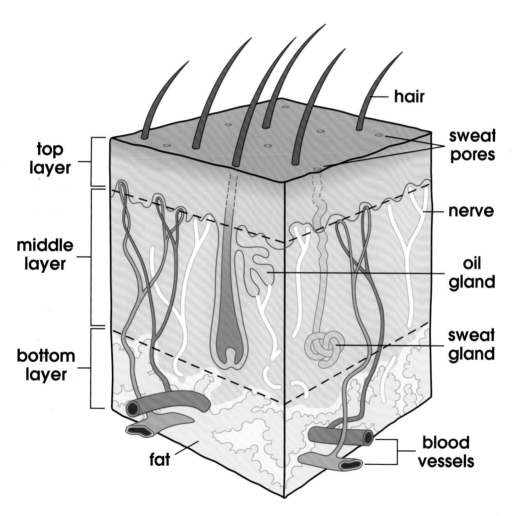

top layer

middle layer

bottom layer

hair

sweat pores

nerve

oil gland

sweat gland

fat

blood vessels

19

# Facts about Skin

 People lose about nine pounds of dead skin cells every year.

 Bat wings are made from skin. The skin is stretched between the long fingers at the ends of their arms.

 Frogs and lizards eat their dead skin to get vitamins.

Some salamanders get air through their skin.

 Oil from a seal's skin keeps its fur waterproof.

 Most brightly colored frogs have a dangerous poison on their skin.

# Glossary

 **camouflaged** – colored to make an animal look like its surroundings

 **protects** – keeps from getting hurt

 **skin** – the outer covering of a person or an animal

 **survive** – to keep living

# Index

The images in this book are used with the permission of: © Hallam Creations/Shutterstock Images, pp. 2, 22 (third from top); © L.E. Baskow/America 24-7/Getty Images, p. 3; © Jonathan Kirn/The Image Bank/Getty Images, p. 4; © Peter Betts/Shutterstock Images, p. 5; © Gerald & Buff Corsi/Visuals Unlimited, Inc., p. 6; © Mayshyphoto/Shutterstock Images, p. 7; © Eric Isselée/Dreamstime.com, p. 8; © David Kuhn, p. 9; © Simon Watson/Stone/Getty Images, p. 10; © S100apm/Dreamstime.com, p. 11; © Mike Severns/Stone/Getty Images, pp. 12, 22 (top); © Todd Pusser/naturepl.com, pp. 13, 22 (second from top); © Louise Murray/Visuals Unlimited, Inc., p. 14; © Ralph H. Bendjebar/Danita Delmont/Alamy, p. 15; © Robert Valentic/Minden Pictures, p. 16; © Paul Springett A/Alamy, pp. 17, 22 (bottom); © Laura Westlund/Independent Picture Service, p. 19.
Front Cover: © Tom Amon/Dreamstime.com

Main body text set in ITC Avant Garde Gothic 21/25. Typeface provided by Adobe Systems.

Lerner Publications Company
A division of Lerner Publishing Group, Inc.
241 First Avenue North
Minneapolis, MN 55401 U.S.A.

Website address: www.lernerbooks.com

Library of Congress Cataloging-in-Publication Data

Boothroyd, Jennifer, 1972–
    Skin / by Jennifer Boothroyd.
        p.    cm. — (First step nonfiction — Body coverings)
    Includes index.
    ISBN 978-0-7613-5789-6 (lib. bdg. : alk. paper)
    1. Skin—Juvenile literature.  I. Title.
QL941.B66  2012
591.47'7—dc22                                            2010050654

Manufactured in the United States of America
1 – PC – 7/15/11